AT
THE
FOOT
OF THE
MOUNTAIN

Mal McKimmie

PUNCHER & WATTMANN

First published in 2021
Published by Puncher and Wattmann
PO Box 279
Waratah NSW 2298

http://www.puncherandwattmann.com
puncherandwattmann@bigpond.com

NATIONAL
LIBRARY
OF AUSTRALIA

A catalogue entry for this book is available from the National Library of Australia.

ISBN   9781925780970

Cover image: Fatata te Moua (At the Foot of a Mountain) by Paul Gauguin
Cover design: Morgan Arnett, with Mal & Lisa McKimmie
Typesetting: Morgan Arnett
Printed by Lightning Source International

This project has been assisted by the Australian Government through the Australia Council, its arts funding and advisory body.

Australian Government

Australia O
Council
for the Arts

Contents

At the Foot of the Mountain

Did I Mention the Dog?

Homunculi

Notes

Acknowledgements

About the Author

*This book is dedicated to Lynette
because it would not exist without her.
If it did, it would be a lesser creation.
As would I.*

I began to address him, saying: "Lord of all virtues, why do you weep?"
And he said to me: "I am like the centre of a circle,
equidistant from all points on the circumference, but you are not."

Vita Nuova, XII, Dante Alighieri, trans. Mark Musa.

At the Foot of the Mountain

The scarabæus was the hieroglyph of the *creator*, the *to be, to become*, to *exist*, the *eternal, the coming into being from chaotic non-being*, also *the itself transforming or becoming*, the *emanating* or *creating* power, also, the *universe*.

SCARABS. *The History, Manufacture and Religious Symbolism of the Scarabæus In Ancient Egypt, Phoenicia, Sardinia, Etruria.*
Isaac Myer, L.L.B.

He cried like the beetle [scarabæus], "O God, My God, look upon me; why hast Thou forsaken Me?"… And a good beetle which with the footprints of virtues twisted the mud of our body, formerly shapeless and sluggish; a good beetle which raises up the poor man from the dunghill.

Exposition of the Holy Gospel according to Saint Luke, Book X, 113.
Ambrose, Bishop of Milan, trans. Theodosia Tomkinson.

When Gregor Samsa woke up one morning from unsettling dreams, he found himself changed in his bed into a monstrous vermin.

also

"Come over here for a minute, you old dung beetle!"

The Metamorphosis, Franz Kafka, trans. Stanley Corngold.

Canto 1

In the middle of the journey of this life
in the Kingdom of Animalia,
after shanking long pilgrimage miles

under a Roman-nosed Tuscan sun,
Dante Alighieri pitched his swag
nell'ombra di una selva oscura

and threw his bag of bones gratefully down;
somewhere nearby, a stream clucked softly in
an admonishing Virgilian tongue.

From a lone spark he kindled a fire.
His medieval teeth stole a white smile
from the Eden graveyard of an apple.

He cracked the dusty spine of Augustine's
Confessiones, and contemplated
the schizoid saint's attitude toward fruit.

Dante fell asleep. Leaves mirrored his fall
until summer lay upon the forest floor
and every tree was winter-penitent.

He fell far from waking and kept on falling
through morphic layer after morphic layer,
inner evolutionary strata.

From one Year of Our Lord to another
he fell; from Jubilee to Jubilee,
Apocalypse to Apocalypse,

Inquisition to Inquisition,
clamouring crowd to incoherent mob.
He fell from riches to poverty,

devolved from phylum, class, order, family,
genus, even species; from the Latin
of *Homo Sapiens*, meaning 'wise man',

he fell, like Francis, into a foolishness,
the hope he sang of in the vulgar tongue
invested elsewhere than his paltry self.

Being the shadow cast by our ideal,
Hell is inside-out and arse-about,
Kafkaesque and scatological.

Haunted to humble, canto by canto,
Dante woke at the foot of the mountain
as one of the insect poor, an exile:

Sisyphus Schæfferi, a dung beetle.

Canto 2

Days pass. Weeks, months, seasons, even years pass.
In a false dawn, the first putative light
of a mythopoeic morning,

his exhaustion seems inexhaustible.
Hell's returnees, no longer sane or same,
have no rehabilitation program

written for them; must write their clumsy own.
After Hell, what makes happening happen?
How did the hill become a mountain,

a towering bookshelf stacked with all his dead,
a wave that rears to tidal, crests and foams
and then refuses steadfastly to break?

He could rest forever in its green shade,
telling himself that the journey's done;
and does rest, for a shell-shocked decade

while the sun ascends by secret route to noon.
Then, like a snow-melt river coursing pure,
il miglior fabbro whispers in his ear:

"Just as there is a hierarchy of sleep,
there is a hierarchy of waking.
The mountain has a spine the eye must climb

from simple sight to the waking vision.
At Hell's centre you found the frozen heart;
at the mountain peak the heart's on fire.

All your feet are fixed feet now: you have been
rebalanced. Increment by increment
you have gathered all your heart's wasted time,

its excrement. Now put your Sisyphean
shoulder to it, push your shit uphill,
every step you take purgatorial."

Dante Alighieri rises, a modern,
a believing disbeliever who must *do*.
He remembers the original vision:

like the seraph that wounded Francis
at the peak of prayer on Mount La Verna,
a creature winged, limned in gold, sacramental:

Scarabæus Sacer, a dung beetle.

Canto 3

The morning sun limns Dante's sleeping form
like an icon, but he wakes feeling far
from iconic. He is more than halfway up

the mountain, closer to destination
than to origin, and sure of nothing.
From thick encircling cloud that hides the peak

his name rings out: the Lord is a child
playing hide-and-seek with the child in him.
Is he ready for that cloud, that child?

Within God's insect the adult mind
still chatters mindlessly about adult things.
To whom? Itself! Despite supplication,

penance, even prayer. It is exhausting.
But he can't go back: becoming 'Dante'
again would be a diminution.

Dante the swooning, unrequited youth,
the inconsolable, the ridiculed.
Dante the soldier, the husband and father,

the man of letters, the respectable.
Dante the prior, the politician,
the White Guelf exiled into the black:

Dante the grey, betrayer and betrayed,
impenitent, peripatetic, proud.
Dante the dead man, the madman, the fool,

who for a taste of Paradise would be
chewed, swallowed, digested by Hell,
then excreted at the foot of this mountain.

All the Dantes he once was, are no more.
They were Caesar's and have been rendered.
His real name is the plaything of that child.

If he returns he'll be an empty shell,
a carapace without a beating heart.
If he returns he'll really be in Hell.

Best to be the best dung beetle he can be!
By God's grace he will be *made* ready.
In Hell he laid his body down, so what

the hell—on this, the purgatorial
mountain, he will lay down his chattering mind.
Under the carapace that he once railed against

are wings itching just for this: for the result
of the result of metamorphosis …
And besides, from the point of view of, say,

an eagle high on the spiral staircase
of a thermal, looking down with its eagle eye,
there is no mountain and no Dante.

There is a circle and a tiny speck crawling
in a halting but inexorable spiral
from the circumference to the centre:

the Love that rolls the sun across the sky.

Did I Mention the Dog?

I may not tell of all the grief I've suffered,
nor do my joyous poems wish to.
Those who love them know in their hearts:
to be reborn such things must be forsaken.

Umberto Saba

Laughter, like sunlight in the cucumber,
The innermost resource, that does not fail.

Norman Cameron

And Then a Cup of Tea

The Captain had a kipper from a previous daring breakfast
Lodged dangerously close to his spine;
But still he led his men.
When he stepped from the wooden dinghy and waded ashore
He was picking his teeth bravely with a fishbone.
The sun rose behind him and broke its yolk upon the New World;
It flowed golden.
Grinning, he dipped his little soldiers in it.

Middle-aged Love Poem

you're sure she has more than just your best interests @heart.com
even if she pities you your age, pedantic grammar &
the blown fuse of your empathy because
these are not confusing times:
so much is known so well in such high definition on such small screens.

your eagerness reveals the luggage you lost @airports.com while
trying to lose your baggage
(she, like a cypher crossed with a zephyr, has neither),
reveals all the books you read @libraries.com, bought @bookshops.com,
all those worlds you didn't invent,
& when you didn't do so, didn't do so *so* unconvincingly—
worlds which now mean what exactly?

you're just one customer in a peak-hour supermarket &
her light is a fluorescent tube's:
when you're in it there's an eagerness to your forgetting that's worrying,
& though it's a worrying easily conquered by forgetting
she's further away each moment because
you're finding it impossible to keep your place
in this sans-serif queue of blogged opinions.

now she's at the checkout & though these lines,
like the headache tablets you passed in aisle 5, are just a distraction
          (including this one)
the headache is very real & so you should turn back.

but you won't. while your actual future
hurtles toward earth like a meteor, you'll wait for her to change,
stand in a dinosaur footprint with your just-bought android smartphone
(on which mainly & with a new species of panic
you kill zombies, are yourself killed, and then resurrect)

until the voices laying daily siege to your hippocampus
broach myriad & reach critical mass &
you're called to decamp from all this packing an aneurysm

a nanosecond after she texts you LOL &
you misread the acronym.

Metastasis
for Alan

Long hours of work are plunged into
as party drunkards might dive into
an empty concrete pool and drown.
This is an Australian mining town.
A white town on black land,
a melanoma on the sun.

More heavy daylight falls than sleep can lighten
and so the metastatic children,
slim and quick as outback lizards,
slip into the night to find
the last drive-in in the world and
the first alcohol.

Afterwards,
the dope and driftwood solace of a beach campfire,
where two bodies writhing puberty away
may shape the shallow grave
of an unintended future;
where a boy sitting alone inside the fire circle

is unaware that his shadow, cast to
man-size by the flames,
is mimicking the firing of a rifle —
he laughs and lifts another bottle, pops the top:
he has his life and name and after all
no grave is ever marked *Suicide By Cop*.

Tomorrow a teenager,
after leaving school for the last time,
will walk into town;
he will stand for too long beside the founder's statue
in the main street
and forget what he was going to say;

he will begin to mouth its lock-jawed yawn,
be dressed in its compliant coat
of thick red dust from neck to knees;
while his sister drifts unnoticed
out through the harbour mouth to where
conjugating seafood writes the sea.

A Reckoning

the Sea shall receive the souls of
the children

receive the souls of
the adults-now-children

into the cradle of its grey arms

and rock and lullaby them
all the long stone underwater road

from storm to becalmed
be calm. Be.

Soon, soon
you, You.

At the breakfast table with your family, perhaps—

before power-point presentations of power
before addresses disregarding the unaddressed
before misrepresentations of the unrepresented—

you, jack-knifed with sudden pain
heartburn and rising bile and brine
surging up into and out of your mouth, the Sea

(the same Sea that cradles boats
 the same Sea that cradles ships
 the same Sea that cradles bones)

the Sea unlocking your snake-jaw at breakfast, you
with your hatred-desire to be empty of everything, you
being emptied by the Sea of its All, you

now dreamless, without history, you
now stranded here forever, you

now an empty shell, a husk, you
now a living ghost, you

now corpse-mouthed at the breakfast table
with your family, perhaps, you

now, you,
now, You.

Villanelle to the Muse from a Disgruntled Poet

That sexy passer-by named History
is love, betrayal, and the keeping score.
Et tu, dark daughter of the singing sea?

I dream of you as if from memory;
then wake, a lonely shipwreck tossed ashore.
Passing by my window, sexy History.

The result of being, like the postman, steady
in blizzard, hailstorm, deluge, gale and more?
Achoo! dark daughter of the singing sea.

Women leave, for with me they feel lonely.
Past the peephole in my apartment door
sashays that sexy gal named History.

I could strike a path to another city!
find there a love whose riches aren't so poor.
Or two, dark daughter of the singing sea.

O cresting wave that breaks—*sometimes*—as poetry,
I reach for you and am cast to the floor.
That passer-by is sexy. You are history.
Adieu, dark daughter of the singing sea.

Moon Mantra

Munificent mark, miracle manna,
Medusa Mary, maenad maelstrom;
Mariner's mainstay, madman's Madonna,
Muse misremembered, myth metronome,
    Mend me magnetically, mine my marrow,
Make my macula manifest mirror;
Map mind's masquerade, mete me my morrow,
Maim me mortally, meeken me, mentor.
    Maladies maggot me, mammon mauls me,
My mephitic metamorphoses mass;
Murdered millions, mourning, mill memory.
    Mare my minotaur, midnight matador,
Marry me mild, my Magdalene mistress;
Mellow mirthful, matrix, my meteor.

Sun Song

Sentient sentinel, Silence-sired sire,
Scarab sans scuttling, Sisyphean stone,
Smiling soliloquy, sly saboteur,
Syzygy's summit, seed Seraphim-sown,
    Stride, Sir! Sneer, snarl, scorn, sotto-sarcastic,
Spurn skyscraper saplings, satellite spin;
Streets soil stigmatic, sour symptomatic:
Swing swords sunbeam-seared—spare sinners, scythe sin.
    Sanity's sideshow stupefies senses:
String summers silken, sacrosanct spider;
Sway softly, sing sweetly, seal spirits saved.
    Symphonic sovereign, soothe self's separateness;
Synchronise skies, smooth seven seas sacred.
School sages! Send saints! Secure soul's surrender.

Thirteen Ways of Not Looking at a Blackbird as a Blackbir

After Wallace Stevens

1.

There are no 'blackbirds with disabilities' — all blackbirds can fly.
There are *only* 'blackbirds with disabilities' — all blackbirds will one day
    fall from the sky.

There is no greater disability than mortality.
What you call my 'disability' is to mortality
as this moment is to Time itself.

All the rest is paperwork.

2.

I once saw a blackbird with a broken wing become roadkill.
It was a hit and run. I saw also
the driver's stricken face.
He was a blackbird.

3.

I tried to convince the psychiatrist that he, too, was a blackbird.
I even gave him a mirror.
He still denied it.

He was nuts.

4.

Four and twenty blackbirds baked in a pie
cannot see outside the pie,
but will eventually all agree that they can.
And agree that it is them out there, free and flying.
And agree even that it is a group of *other* blackbirds
who are trapped in the pie:
four and twenty blackbirds who deserve it.

These principles apply to blackbirds
as well as blackbirds.

5.

You do not know
that the feather in your cap
signifies either a suicide or a murder.

6.

Dante was a blackbird who flew higher than most because
he was willing to descend into his blackness.
After he did that, he ascended into his birdness.
And after he did that, he transcended both blackness and birdness,
even if only for a moment.

7.

There is no word for the immensity of Sky.

For some blackbirds
the sky is full of fear and madness. About to fall.
No-one has ever told them that they are blackbirds,
that the sky is there for *them*,
that it will not fall, that they can fly up into it,
that everything is the other way around.

Who will tell them?

8.

I once sat in the back seat of a car
between a blind blackbird and a deaf blackbird.
The blind blackbird couldn't see what the deaf blackbird signed,
and the deaf blackbird couldn't hear what the blind blackbird said.

I became the eyes of one and the ears of another.
And they flew together.
And I flew with them.

9.

They say that Jesus wasn't a blackbird. Of course he was.
He was black as night.
That is why they crucified him; then told us that he rose white.

Don't believe them.
They're blackbirds, all of them.

10.

I have known and know many blackbirds that you call
'blackbirds with disabilities' (I am one of them).
I have known and know many blackbirds that you have diagnosed
as having a 'blackbird illness' (I am one of them).

I refuse to use these terms about any blackbirds, even you.
What do you call them then? you ask me.

(You are a blackbird that doesn't know it is a blackbird
speaking about other blackbirds
with a blackbird that knows it is a blackbird.
If only you knew, you little blackbird, you!)

I call them Maria and Paolo and Dennis and David and Julie and
Susan and Craig and Millie and Angela and Wendy and Roger and
Kelvin and Dion and ...

and I'll be damned if I know why you don't.

11.

You're looking for a collective noun
that won't insult blackbirds?

You should probably try flight.

No, not the word you idiot! The act!

12.
The City of Dis is a hell-on-earth
that blackbirds created for other blackbirds.
No-one remembers when hell-on-earth
became the only earth there is.
No-one remembers when we all fell from the sky.

But everyone is freezing here,
trapped under inexplicable ice at the centre of the inferno,
frozen with our wings stretched out
as if we are flying.

Frozen with our beaks open
as if we are talking about these things,
as if we have not obeyed the injunction
that we ourselves wrote, and so have not
abandoned all hope.

13.
I'm sorry.
I cannot help you.

I'm just a blackbird.
Remember?

Plasterica! Plasterica!

Yet as I gazed from the deck at the surface of what ought to have been a pristine ocean, I was confronted, as far as the eye could see, with the sight of plastic.
Capt. Charles Moore, discoverer of the Great Pacific Garbage Patch

In the dream is a room; in the room is an ocean.
Floating on the ocean is a bed—it is your deathbed.
You lie on it alone & discarded—disconnected.

Between you & the horizon is a country with the ambitions
of a continent. It is so close you might have casually tossed it
piece by piece from the bed; if you were still able to move,
you could reach out & stroke its polymer shoreline as if it were a pet.

Your last rattling breath quickens the dance in slanting light
of all the skin cells you have ever shed—almost a whole person's worth!
You watch them come together, coalesce into
a blind & featureless simulacrum, a golem that turns away &

strides ashore to plant a flag & claim a future—your job is done.
A plastic seagull lands upon the bed & pecks your eyes out.
You dream of a room; in the room is an ocean.

An Antisocial Medium Writes an Antisonnet
written after turning down a request

'Publishing' on Instagram a sonnet
that explores the theme of mental health
is like making levees out of blocks of ice
as floodwaters rise on a warming planet,

or like engraving the mind-numbing phrase
'Guns don't kill people, people kill people'
on the barrel of a semi-automatic.
So I met with a friend in the park & we

talked politics and pets: WHAT'S hAPPening
in the world, dogs versus cats. We were there,
right there, INSTAnt, unGRAMatical, loud.

Later, in the shade of a red gum mansion
inhabited by TWITTERing rosellas,
we sat side by side, our FACEs in BOOKs,

unashamedly elite and quietly sane;
knowing that what we need is within words
said, written or read, or just (just!) within.

I, Incitatus

A fair horse, almost divine,
It strode majestically into the hall,
Greeted everyone with due regard,
Taking no notice of rank, or office, or even of the ministers,
And went straight to its appointed place,
Modestly,
As if it were ashamed of being there.

Rudolf Marku

I, Incitatus,
broken and bridled
equine senator,
steed to a self-deified
emperor, strode the equator
at the hand of my master,
left the whole world
gasping for breath.

In the unofficial version
of the divine birth legend
Caligula, the Once-born, rises
hydrocephalic and insane
from the morning vomit
of his father, Bacchus.

Death is foretold in his eyes:
he already knows
he will inherit an empire.
Darkness riots in his veins
like wine long turned to vinegar:
the future is an ecstasy turned sour.

When Caligula's assassins descended
like the Furies upon him,
wielding a death he could not outride,
nothing changed.

I, Incitatus,
coupling with new masters,
still, daily, circle the globe,
villages, cities, whole histories
devoured by fires sparked by my hooves
and fanned by the wind of my passing.

Between times,
in the cool night,
sleeping standing in my ivory manger,
I dream of my name being called
by a real God, twice-born:

an ecstatic God of women,
children and animals,
calling me to freedom.

For nothing changes.
I am a Horse and my
ancestors were Horses.

I remember Dionysus.

Chaos Theory

Chaos theory is theory about order:
chaos is merely perceived.

That violent storm that with its sting
scuttled black-bellied across the sky like a scorpion
then paused above me in the middle of my day
in the middle of my life
& then eclipsed the sun

began, so they say, on the far side of the earth
when a butterfly dreaming it was a man
moved ever so slightly its theoretical wings.

This butterfly of theory is,
as the births of many gods long ago were
& the death of one god more recently was,
evidence of a new ordering of things.

  Or it is not

For unlike storms, theories, & beliefs,
gods, butterflies, & their wings
seem to always exist on the far side of the earth.

Now that I am stung, I have the storm inside me.
What is left for me here where gods & wings are not?
What is left for me under the sun?

I have to leave now for the far side of the earth;
I'll see you if & when I return.

I'm sure I will dream of you while I am there
But because I love you so
I will try not to move in my dream, even minutely,
a single finger in greeting.
Who knows what could happen?

Until I return then, Hello!

The Sleeping
After Theodore Roethke

I slept to wake and took my waking fast.
Mine was my fate and so I had no fear.
What could I learn by dwelling on the past?

We feel to think: the mind is all that lasts.
I heard my smartphone ringing in my ear
And woke from sleep and took my waking fast.

You lay beside me, that was all I asked
O lovely body I left dreaming there.
What could we learn by dwelling on the past?

Night filled the day, like dark wine fills a glass:
My heart gave way upon my office stair.
From sleep a waking took me far and fast.

Now Nature has a different kind of task
for you to do: breathe deep the living air,
but don't forget me dwelling in your past.

You shed one tear; my best friend sheds his mask.
I fall away from always. But am near!
I watch you as you take your waking fast.
I watch you never dwelling on the past.

His Life as a Sonnet

Me,
You?
   Yes
Oh!

You,
Him?
   Yes
No!

   Bye
Wait!
   What?
Why?

   Ohhhhhhhhhhh
Oh.

Blue Phenomena

The death of Satan was a tragedy
For the imagination. A capital
Negation destroyed him in his tenement
And, with him, many blue phenomena.
          Esthétique du Mal, Wallace Stevens

The dolphin is not Platonic. There is no Idea of dolphin.
Dolphin is one of the names of the Utterly Real.
Put your ear to sea—clicks and clacks, chirps and whirrs and whistles:
not dialectic, but dialogic.

The dolphin's smile is involuntary, fixed,
is Darwin's wry mandible: the dolphin is not smiling.
Not at me, not at you.
The earth is not a bright blue ball
spinning in a themed amusement park.

The Aristotelian dolphin breathes voluntarily,
which is to say consciously, objectively.
Even in sleep its brain,
30 percent larger than a human's, 40 million years older,
is always partly awake,
hemispheres napping in turns like
the parents of a newborn.
If the dolphin fully sleeps, it drowns.

There can be no forgetting.

There is no moment for the dolphin but the moment it is in.
The Sea is always where it is and Home.

ʕ

I had already visited the desert,
which is to say, the Sky,
had, indeed, almost lost myself there.
I knew that the Sea was heretical too.
But how could I refuse my Mother's call?
I didn't hesitate for a moment. I ran and dived into the blue.

I swam with seals twice.
I swam with dolphins many times.
Once I swam alongside whales:
two Southern Rights, a mother and her calf.

What can I say?
Seals are like children, mischievous and darting, unconsciously graceful.
A whale seems the Sea itself incarnate, seems a God.
Dolphins, like adults who have become truly whole,
are somewhere in between.

We pretend we love the great saints
but we fear that they will kill us;
that in their arms we will be overwhelmed, will drown,
die as named individuals within Creation.

But we forget that they are lovers and breathe
as willingly and consciously as dolphins:
in their arms we are revived
to nameless Creation within the individual.

I would like to swim with Orcas,
(Killer Whale is a misnomer:
they are actually the largest of the dolphin family).
I would like to swim with them, and do not believe
they would hurt me.
But then again, I'm a fool. I dive straight in.

❧

As if guiding an ailing ship to safe harbour,
dolphins cured me forever of religion.
I have become a happy heretic,
an objective citizen of the world that I live in.
For Lent I gave up giving up and then I gave up Lent.
I stole Augustine's stolen pears and ate them as an early breakfast,
refusing to confess, refusing to repent.

Original sin is unoriginal. Pears are juicy.
The gate to the City of God swings open and shut
somewhere in the blinkered riddle
of this human mind and body.

East and West are identical twins who at first glance and at second
do not appear even to be siblings.
At the third glance everything changes:
each looks at the other as if looking for the first time in a mirror.
The differences between them matter, do not matter:
they are two halves of a whole, were once an undivided egg.

What do I care if I do or don't have a past or a future life?
What do I care if there is or isn't a Heaven or a Hell?
I am swimming in the purgatorial, phenomenal Now.
And it is every possible shade of blue.

ᕫ

The miracle of the Buddha's enlightenment
was not his near-death asceticism or his heroic final meditation
but the witnessing Earth which,
when he touched it at the vital moment
(having been challenged by Mara, the Demon king,
to provide a witness to his awakening)
sang for him as the spheres sing—myriad voices as a single voice.

Without the love of the wide-awake and waiting Earth
he would have died (perhaps then and there
in the sacred shade of the sacred tree)
Siddhartha Gautama.
But he rose to his mendicant feet The Buddha.

The miracle of the cross was not
that Jesus's last breath rhymed perfectly
(because willingly, consciously, objectively) with death,
that his final exhalation had an embrace so wide, so utter and entire,
that there was air to spare to sing the resurrection of the Christ;
nor even that resurrection.

The miracle of the cross was the gull guano at its foot,
the view clear and cloudless to a horizon where a single dolphin leapt,
over and over and over,
a silver needle stitching Sea to Sky, Sky to Sea,
repairing, without embellishment or artifice, the Real.

To My Children

Now that I am
to some extent free
of I & my & mine & me
& so of certain hopes & certain laments
I can write this apology

though it is not enough
not nearly enough

for you, my children who never existed
who never played & sang & ran & wept & laughed
& shall never do so.

I am so, so sorry.

I had a choice, yes,
even if it seemed no choice at all:

the house was burning
& the people in it
& I had to enter
so great was my love for them,
my sons & my daughters.

(If I had not entered
would I have been able
to live with the guilt?
Perhaps your non-existence
was guaranteed
no matter the outcome.)

Nonetheless, I am sorry,
& sometimes,
missing you & who you
might have been & become,
I feel a regret
almost beyond measure.

Forgive me that I chose
my sons & daughters in
the burning present
over you, my sons & daughters in
the burning future.

Show mercy in your judgement.

40 Days & 40 Nights

Noah was afraid
even before he received instructions from the Lord.

When he looked through his window,
poked his head out of his door,
left his house,
wandered about in the world,
he was afraid.
He was afraid for the people living;
he was particularly afraid for those to come.

Noah was afraid
even after he received instructions from the Lord.

He was afraid every day during
the many painstaking years it took
to build the ark;
as he herded the animals onto it
two by two,
a process that seemed to take forever;
as he boarded his wife and sons &
his son's wives.

Noah was afraid
when he felt the first raindrop on his skin,
& the second, & the third.

But then he saw that within every raindrop,
smaller than a grain of rice &
curled like a bean,
was an unborn child,
miniscule, perfect & unique,
perfect *because* unique,
its eyelids flickering with dream.

Noah laughed for 40 days & 40 nights.

The Chamber

Whose wings are these that brush me in this dark?
The sentry at my tomb has stamped a heel.
Is there a heart inside the human heart?

From fitful life I wake in fits and starts,
As wolves from dreams of snow wake to snow's chill.
Whose wings are these that brush me in this dark?

My pulse of pain follows the lunar chart:
When wolves are snared they have the mouth of howl.
Is there a heart inside the human heart?

Of breathless space my breath becomes a part:
Wolves trapped by death make of themselves a meal.
Whose wings are these that brush me in this dark?

To free myself I tear myself apart:
The wolf escapes three-legged from the steel.
Is there a heart inside the human heart?

The sentry stands aside. This savage art
has saved me from myself—the tomb is still.
I have been brushed by those wings in that dark;
have seen inside the human heart a heart.

Why Homeopathy Is Not a Science

Once upon a time I did not exist, did not know pain,
threading darkness through the needle-eye of zero.
But love is made and makes us:
we are born and broken.

Love leaves, returns, leaves, and then returns again,
a prodigal; a recurring dream that sleep cannot sustain.
Treading softly as the light, it wakes us
day by day and pain by pain,
until *nothing left to lose, everything to gain*
is an idiot heart's loudly sung refrain.

'Bedding lovers filled with love's light breaks us,'
he weeps, afterwards.
                    'But love will break this brokenness back again:
a drug that leaps from artery to vein
spreading light throughout the body, it takes us
incrementally but wholly,' she promises.
                              Aloud, he reads: 'As pain
and cure for pain, love takes each moment's strain.'

'Shedding darkness we are light,' she recites in reply.

                              Poets are vain:
wedding vows should not be written by them; or not written. Love shakes us
empty then we're old, and words are broken back again
as memory … How much can hearts contain,
dreading darkness and the night? And parents? Love forsakes us
always and eventually
                    (but the sea diluted to a millionth part in one rain-
drop held under the tongue is like curing like, pain curing pain,
love slowly breaking our brokenness back again

New Year Bee Prayer
for Elizabeth & Robert

May this year
close its eyes

May this sweet year
enter quietly the past;

May the good bees
honeycomb its carcass;

with the dawn
one by golden one

And may this swarm
as does the sun

to cast in light
(We hive our

Love's wings and stings
May next year

be sweet as years can be.
with the Queen;

three-sixty-five
be honeywise

when it is done
lay itself down.

when it must
may this year pass.

of Aristaeus
may they swell its belly

as moments do & dreams:
until a swarm.

rise ripe, renewed
whose name is Love

all time-to-come.
duty honey where

flotsam a shore.)
because of bees

May you find shelter
may every day

be honeycombed
and hum your honey names.

Retirement Triptych

1. A Toast

The Best Poet in the Language,
wherever he is,
has a Gorbachev birthmark in the shape of your country
on his phrenological forehead.
You are introduced to him and it flushes cab-sav:
suddenly, you are head-over-heels inebriated.

This is seal and signifier from the Gods of second births:
critics have shot him straight into the canon,
an *a priori* trick that even the satirical clowns bow down to,
weeping on their inconsolable shoes.

He strides, he bounds!
up to the dais, the podium
(his every ringing step improves us)

or, deferential not to status but to image,
shuffles halo-humbled to the microphone
(his every halting step includes us)

arranges his books and papers: New Poems!
"upon a lectern rustic, unembellished"
(as he later writes, reflecting)

arranges his books and papers, thus himself:
he is both essence and extension, the body and the body-politic
(every word, every drop, from his lips)

clears his vine-throat, clucks his grape-tongue,
opens his wine-mouth and pours: "I …

2. All Our Pretty Horses

the poets of the new century
trot in on their shiny white ponies

(they might be ponies, but at least they're white)

The poets of the new century
trot in on their shiny white ponies
young male poets in the lead

(they might be young but at least they're male)

the poets of the new century
trot in on their shiny white ponies
young male poets in the lead
followed by young female poets

(they might be female, but at least they're young)

The poets of the new century
trot in on their shiny white ponies
young male poets in the lead
followed by young female poets
heralded by old male critics

(they might be old, but at least they're there)

The poets of the new century
trot in on their shiny white ponies
young male poets in the lead
followed by young female poets
heralded by old male critics
and herded by old male anthologists

(they might be anthologists, but at least there's a last line to this poem)

3. Did I Mention the Dog?

I wasn't a poet in a gaggle of poets
or whatever the collective noun may be.

I was just a guy who, while out taking a walk,
ran into a group of people, nice people generally,
most more interesting at first glance than at second;
a handful of cracking sorts on the outskirts of the group
& at the centre some prime arseholes.
(If any in the second category are reading this
I'm sure they think they're in the first).

I met them & got distracted from my path.
By the words & ideas & the wit & the beers & yes, a woman or two.
I felt, often, in the midst of all the
opinions & drinking & knowing & neuroses, all the desperation,
like a charlatan.

I realise now that I cared far less than I pretended to:
a *lot* less than I pretended to.
I was just a guy who was distracted while out walking the dog.

Did I mention the dog? I really loved that dog.
His name was Whitman & he was happiest when rolling in the grass.

I'm off now to find him.
I hope he's still alive, I hope he still loves me,
that he doesn't feel as abandoned as I feel ashamed.

See you later then.
It was … it was … distracting.
I did laugh a fair amount, so there's that.

I hope you liked the poems.

Homunculi

something bizarre about Henry, slowly sheared
off, unlike you & you,

smaller & smaller, till in question stood
his eyeteeth and one block of memories

Op. posth. no. 1 (Dream Song 78), John Berryman

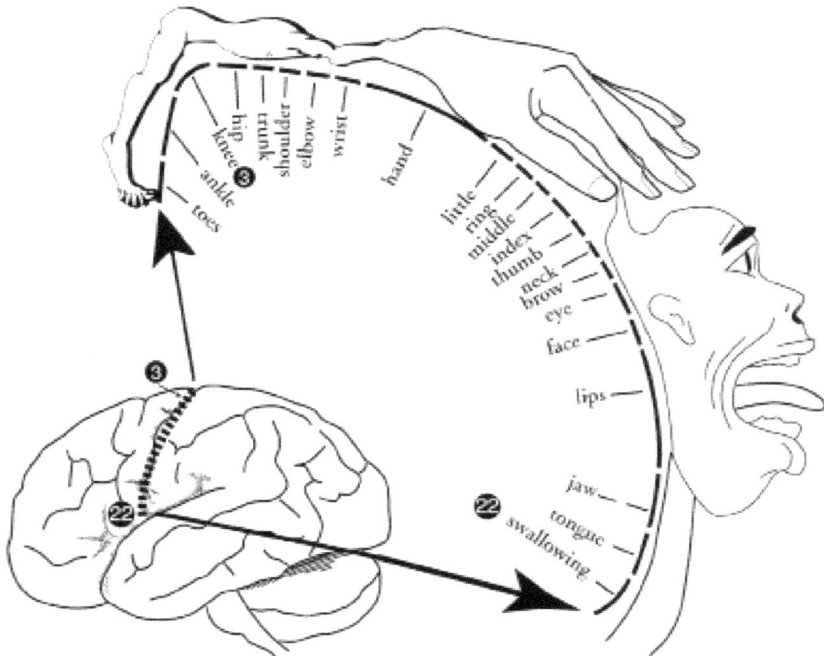

Heraldic

You say everything with the confidence of other people's wisdom,
such as, *God is the illness I would most like to die from.*
You are a fool.

The man who chose joy over happiness
may have suffered more than most,
knowing not what he had chosen,
but knowing exactly what he had not.

Tonight I am a shadow in a marble palace,
flitting from pillar to pillar.

It is Easter. I put my left hand in the sea to complete the circle.
It is Easter. The Magdalene is moving like a mermaid underwater.
It is Easter. Time to nail to a wooden mast a river and set sail.

You are far away; the hospital is closer.

Intelligence Report:
A rogue poet is making weapons grade poetry
from the spent fuel cells in his heart.

Be assured that I love you;
I was listening only to the first part of your question.

Because even the dead cannot completely become effect,
I may as well keep on causing.

When Job with foresight met Job with hindsight...
God happened.

The Misanthrope's Question:
Am I an optimist or a pessimist?
Is the world half-full or half-empty of bastards?

In the grip of the death-cure I plead for normal.

Lunching at the Hare Krishna restaurant,
I was told that I am not this body.
But then, I am not a Hare Krishna.

All is suffering, said the Buddha. Then he smiled.
All is Joy, said the Christos. Then he wept.

My life does not conform to the backstory I was born with.
As far as I know.

How to reconcile poetry with
my almanac of golden saints; book of icons;
the deep, lost purple of the archetypes?

Here, soon, simply in the company of friends,
there will be a vertical opening in the air.

Individual results may vary.

Call a doctor if irritation persists.

Hospital

In a dream the Turin Shroud
is being laundered in the bowels of Hospital;
I wake knowing how to prove it a fraud.

Morning again. Unavoidable as virus in vapour
or the breeding of bacteria.

'This is Lazarus.
I need an outside line.'

When my family came to visit I was asleep, dreaming
that my family came to visit.

Let us play, child, the game of crucifixion:
Pin the heart on the skeleton.

Doctor: *Who told you to go off your antidepressants?*
Patient: *My body told my brain, my brain told my mind,*
my mind told my soul, my soul told me.
Doctor: *For how long have you been hearing these voices?*

My tongue is a dry stone in a dry riverbed.
My bad brain banging in its skull bucket is a sponge.
My mind is water wrung out & returned to the sea.

I flirt with the beautiful nurse.
In Hospital's mirror: The Bearded Lady weds The Hanged Man.
Again.

Against medical advice, & sans medication,
my words discharge themselves—Shall I follow them?
If I leave now, can I catch up with them?

A ship in a bottle is a hobby. The sea in a bottle is art.
A ship in the sea in a bottle is prayer.
A man in the ship in the sea in the bottle is praying that art
does not become a hobby.

2 AM … my sleeping next-bed neighbour, 80-year-old Bob,
whose wife visits him all-day & daily,
cries out from our common dream: *Where have you gone?*

I hope that next time the idiot intern
finds my vein so I can strangle him with it.

Visitors gurn their faces against the aquarium glass—
see the deep-sea fish in shallow water,
the lamps on stalks futile on their foreheads!

Outside—a summer's day.
Here, inside the god's bicep, lightning leaping from strata to strata.

I have found him out: he *fears* the skull opened,
the can of worms revealed as one long, beautiful,
convoluted worm …

I will be a spy in enemy territory.
Death and I have synchronised our watches.

Twice the abyss awakened & stared at me with my own eyes.
The third time, this time,
they weren't my eyes.

Are we there yet?
Are we there yet?
Are we there yet?

Fish are subatomic physicists, separating O from H2O.
(I saw them doing it.)

In sight of Iolkos, carrying the Golden Fleece,
Jason & his crew almost foundered on a hidden reef …
How on earth will I cope, on earth, with this grief?

Again the citizens have staged a referendum
that Life has won by the smallest of margins …
How can I campaign in the swing state if I don't know where it is?

Smell is Memory.
Here, we are downwind from our futures only,
in these hospital gowns from which bare arses hang.

Trials have ceased because of an unacceptable number
of patient deaths.

Leave me be. Go & ask the newborn child
what it's *really* like in the womb.

His & Hers

When I knocked on your door & you opened it smiling
the beam in your eye
knocked me & my mote flying.

Assured you were a placebo & I was in the control group
I took part in this experiment.
It was all a lie—I have the symptoms to prove it.

In the morning I will tell her how a fat, buzzing, blowfly-yellow moon
flew into the car & beat its wings against the windscreen
while I drove through the night to her door.

This morning I opened my door to the conclusions of Loss:
bouquets of poems, a tideline of foam-white flowers.
I wonder when I will meet the lover who sends them to me from the future

Be forever dead in Eurydice, Rilke advised.
Berryman thought Rilke needed to 'get down into the arena and kick around'
(Henry said Rilke was a jerk.)

Would I love you if Neruda did not write:
Quiero hacer contigo lo que la primavera hace con los cerezos
(I want to do with you what spring does with the cherry trees)?

Orgasm, a scopolamine moment:
briefly, as in a police line-up,
all the usual suspects.

'You are not alone' the Goddess sang, dancing around my grave.
And finally I heard the legend of *Eurydice's* head.

In the dream, the fact that I was dead
enabled me to write the poem
that I gave to the beautiful woman.

In the language of the deaf the sign for *beautiful* is beautiful,
the sign for *calm* is calming,
& *love* & *happy* each require a hand & a heart to be invoked.

Shy man, 45, GSOH, NS, SD, Tourette's syndrome,
seeks beautiful woman 18-25, GSOH, NS, SD, Echolalia.

Her: *Poetry is like sex, it goes round & round;*
that's why I'll hang on with you.
Him: *So I'm a good poet, but a bad lover?*

Curse the prosaic who reduce the aim from loving to living,
from O! to I. (Diminishing even punctuation.)

Only if I move this glass paperweight
will the snowflakes inside it fall soft as syllables
on her dress, her upturned face, her hair.

In the hospital-fever nightmare, her father was the attending doctor
handing her not the child but the placenta
& ordering that it be raised to adulthood.

The lonely man with his ear to a drinking glass against
the apartment wall;
not to hear his neighbour's words, just to know she's there.

Her: *Aieeeearrrgh!! %$#*+@*%$#*+%@!!*
Him: *We're having a baby! We're having a baby!*

The world is imperilled because men were once children.
The world will continue because women were once children.

You were a 5' 6" upturned hourglass; we were in my kitchen;
& all the women I had ever loved
passed before me one by one
while I cooked a perfect egg.

Homunculus

My mother, 8 months pregnant, wakes to blood.
In dire emergency she overhears a doctor say, *This baby's dead.*
        My first misdiagnosis!
& the beginning of my long battle with doctors & with death.

While around it adults debate the nature of the afterlife,
half the child is, half the time, still half-in the place
where it lived before it was born
(now is the beginning of its self-division).

The men who created the world created the Devil.
But the world is not the Earth & I created the Earth for you.
God whispers this O so quietly in the ear of every newborn child.
Then—the clamour of our welcome.

What did I dream in the womb for those 8 months?
What dreams would I have had in the 9th?
Can I have them now & so change the past?

Some children are too large to live in the tiny space allotted them
without hurting themselves or others.
Because they love others, they choose to hurt themselves.

Adults diagnose the children
who fail at becoming adults
in a world created by adults
who were once children trying not to fail at becoming adults.

An apple flames red on the windowsill.
The hungry child eats it & is eaten by
the haggard, ravenous suburb prowling around outside.

See the child running away in the night, leaping like a flame from roof to roof.
You fear for him—he is running in the dark toward the sea.
You are looking at it wrongly—he is running toward the rising sun.

They told him all about his future,
how rosy it was & how much better than his present.
Why did he believe them?
They were from the land of Television, where all his friends lived.

There is no *CSI Childhood,*
even if later it feels like there were clues scattered everywhere.

Climate Change is the accumulation of everything unsaid.
In the car seat the child adopts the pose
of a post-test crash test dummy.

We exit one womb & enter another.
Creation is the womb of the Mother of all our mothers
& this is how we treat her.
No wonder we die howling like children.

What does it matter that this poem isn't longer,
that I can remember so little of what others call my childhood?
Tell me about yours—& don't leave anything out!

P.S.
Sorry about the bloody footprints on the mat at the front door.
It still says WELCOME.

Haloperidol

Because I hesitated at the threshold of phenomena,
because I turned to run away,
my body was born with my mind on backwards.

The nurse is telling me about the half-life of Haloperidol.
I can't hear her for the geiger-counter swarm of cicadas
in my Chernobyl meltdown of a head.

At the admissions desk I give the name Gregor Samsa
but it has already been taken by some other vermin.

This is Galileo's vacuum.
Diagnosed, we are all falling at the same speed,
the weight of our individual pasts irrelevant.

When they agreed I could make a fort out of the furniture
I agreed to stay.

How many people, in trying to help others,
are really trying to heal their own deeply hidden wounds?
I went mad out of compassion for psychiatrists.

Head of-Orpheus, this is Head-of-John-the-Baptist;
Head-of-John-the-Baptist, this is Head-of-Orpheus.
I can't believe you two haven't met each other!

Graffiti in the toilets:
The Special Theory of Relatives: E =MC²
Empathy = Medication x Condescension² (condescension is always squared).
        Einstein wasn't here

They tell me it's delusion, this belief that my body is an urn full of ashes.
So I go & perch on the mantelpiece.

They have turned on the influencing machine again, he says.
It is removing the thoughts from my head & replacing them.
It's using rays or beams or something …
They increase his meds & sit him in front of the TV.

It's not that everyone here believes in Original Sin,
many are not even religious.
It's that everyone here believes in Original Sinners.

Birth is a process, not an event.
I was just trying to finish the process.
Unfortunately I was judged an adult at the time.

I don't believe in the Devil, God's opposite,
I believe in the palindromic dog,
man's howling, growling, leg-humping best friend.

That ghostly head in the CT scan?
It sits atop my neck.

I no longer know whether human beings gave birth to the myths
or the myths to human beings.
Nurse—hand me my stilts!

Graffiti in the toilets:
They gave me this felt pen so I wouldn't use my own excrement.
What do they think writing is?
ps. I'll be damned if I sign my name using their pen.' ▉ ▉

The pattern in the carpet ebbs & flows.
His head floats down the corridor, buzzing like a bee.
They tore it from his body while trying to find his sting.
They should have looked under his tongue.

For all I know, the psychiatrist who is delving into my denial
lives with his wife & kids in a beautiful house with the sea at its door
& does not believe in climate change.

If you can't play a practical joke in a psychiatric ward, where can you?

My psychosis was a one-page letter I scrawled to myself as a child.
I didn't know how to mail it, so just slid it under my bed.
It grew there into *War and Peace, Crime and Punishment.*

This is the shore onto which Lucifer fell from his high station.
I lie on my back & make sand-angels.

Graffiti in the women's toilets:
Out of sight   Out of mind.
Out of [His] sight   Out of [her] mind.

It took a long, long time for the humidicrib to become the bell jar.
Even so, lined up outside the glass:
family, doctors, nurses—the usual suspects.

You worked so hard at not thinking certain thoughts
that I found myself thinking them for you.
Your shadow seemed so lonely that I let it accompany mine.

The mirror within me is shattered into a thousand pieces.
Still, *still,* reflected in every shard—my individual face.

In the courtyard, I cadge a smoke from Mary, the Mother of God,
who is suffering from post-partum depression.
How dark it was when the Logos left her!

I had a visitor today.
Or he thought I did.

Give me a bucket for my tears:
I am going to make a sandcastle for the King!

It really shouldn't be this easy to tell
that the psychiatrist also wants to leave his body.

If only I could have looked at my watch when I was born!

The psychiatrist tells me that he can believe in Beauty & Truth, but not in God.
I tell him that if he falls on his knees before Beauty & Truth
everything will change.

When I returned from madness
I dug a hole & buried every volume of philosophy I owned
in the very same earth that chewed me up, then spat me out.

Even though this all happened a long time ago
it was only recently that I realised
this all happened a long time ago.

Don't worry if now I speak of the future as if it's the present.
It may be confusing, but it's harmless—it's only hope.

Someone pitied me just the other day.
I forgave him, the poor fellow.

Heretical

When I realised that transcendental experiences happen
only to those who have not transcended,
I left to seek the company of one who had.

There is a God that exists only in your question:
Do you believe in God? & nowhere else.
I do not believe in that God & so
without lying can answer *No*.

Hold fast!
The tunnel exists because of the light at the end of it.
It is not the other way round.

The Goddess said to me:
Don't desire Shaktipat. It is transient.
Desire me, Shakti. I am eternal.

I'm sorry, your book sounds nice,
but my reading has been interrupted, perhaps forever:
God is now more important to me than a fictional character.

I have no time for priests (my Heaven is between me & my God).
I have no time for psychiatrists (so is my Hell).

Any God that has form & attributes
is but a form & attribute
of the God who has neither form nor attributes.

The skulls of infallible popes
are necklaced round the throat of the Goddess.

The world is full of people who avoid people with wounds.
They do this because of their own wounds.
(The world is full of people with wounds.)

Every time I take the Lord down from the cross
I wrestle him from my arms & I put him back up there.
I will never stop trying to take him down, even if I won't let me.

I once asked a Catholic priest this question:
"Given the *Father* & the *Son,* what is the gender of the Holy Spirit?"
I did not receive an answer.

I would apologise for my silence,
but how can I when it is God who has bitten my tongue?

The Goddess said to me: *I may seem far away,*
my words making their way to you down a long tunnel.
But that tunnel is your body. That is how close I am.

Prepare yourself for darkness O my soul!
The Lord may have left you with a broken chariot,
but the Lord arrives in a chariot whole.

I worship at the Church of the Sacred Ambidextrous Heart
(heart half underwater & half above),
kneeling before the Centre-of-Things.

Arjuna's grief is beyond human measurement.
Only Krishna, being its cure,
can plumb its depth.

I abandoned hope but did not abandon faith.
Hope walks in polished Italian leather shoes;
faith wanders about in all weathers happily discalced.

I place all my watches, diaries, clocks & calendars
at the lotus feet of the Lord.
Tick tock, says my mind, *tick tock*.

Yes, there is a limit to your depths;
but that which is the limit
has no limit to *its* depths.

There is Earth & there is Heaven.
In between is the purgatorial mountain.
All else is human invention.

The outraged townspeople picketed the building of a Catholic church:
they didn't want terrorism in their community.
Some of those who had been terrorised as children, & survived,
now had children of their own & were terrified for them.

I could no longer stand the loss of Christ-in-the-world:
everywhere the crucified Christ, nowhere the resurrected Christ.
Easter isn't once a year. Easter is every moment of every day.

Milked from the fangs of the Laughing Snake Goddess:
an antivenin to cure those bitten
by a deadly serious religion.

Disciple: *It is this body that prevents my return to the ocean.*
Guru: *It is this body that allows my daily return.*

I *know* I can't take my wealth over the threshold.
Why does no-one ever say the same about my health?

The way is narrower than the single hair the prideful monk
purposefully leaves when shaving his head.
Leaving that, he may as well live fully in the world.

The soul is an organ waiting for a body transplant
& may reject the transplanted body.

In the name of the Mouth, the Tongue, & the Holy Word.
Om, Aum, Amen, Amin, Nam, Name.

Beware! The Known is becoming The Written.
Beware! The Written is becoming The Taught.
Beware! The Taught is becoming The Believed.
Beware! The Believed is becoming The Law.

Knock Knock Knock! … Ah it's you. Hello again.

Hopeful

A long time ago I opened a can of worms.
I had no choice but to go fishing.
By happy accident, I hooked the Sea itself.

This new line on the palm of my writing hand appeared just the other day.
I think it is the horizon.

Don't be in such a hurry; there's a war on somewhere every day.
After all, what do you have to pack for war?
You are already wearing your life!

Just yesterday I thought:
I live now with experiences for which I have no explanation.
But then I realised:
I always have.

Being more than halfway out of who I was
(disregarding the pain)
I am more than halfway into who I am.

I suffer from a number of illnesses you do not & will never have.
No, don't thank me. You're welcome.

I found out that the desert is a conch shell when,
on my last legs,
I let go, lay down, & so put my ear to it.

Amputate your writing arm; it will grow back.
If it doesn't, don't worry—in this world, a phantom limb
often writes better poetry.

Now that the ceiling has lifted & the house is open to the sky
I have no home.
I am, as I have always felt—a passer-by.

My heart beats on as if
there is nothing wrong with me,
as if upside-down is the heart's right-side-up.

Habit is a hell of a thing:
even though I'm no longer in Hell,
I keep forgetting that I'm happy.

I dig up Darwin's skull & it is laughing.
Its laughter quickens my evolution.

Two love-birds, or birds in love, once nested in my wound.
Soon, soon, all the birds will return.
Storm clouds will be dispersed by storm clouds.

Farewell! I am emigrating to
The Land Without Autobiography,
where everybody says *thou* before they say *I*.

Cheer up fella!
The other parts of your life are parts
of other people's lives.

O to be reborn under a star
that you *know* is still alive when its light reaches you!

The sand that falls in the hourglass here, lands elsewhere.
Time is making, grain by grain, another shore.

The Sky is one wing of the Angel, the Sea the other.
I have built for us a boat entirely of feathers.

The branch from which Judas swung
is bare now but for a hive in which
the consorts of the Queen are busy humming Her name.

The still, small voice is no longer still & small.
It says these things so that they may happen.

The Sun has risen as a woman.
Now I understand why the man in the moon was hysterical.
       O you fool!
How is the mirror diminished when the light is Hers?

See those motes of dust dancing in that beam of light?
I am one of them!
There is no doubt, not a mote's worth!

Yes, there is still a great rent in the sky.
But can't you see that now
there are flowers falling through it?

Notes

Cover Image

This painting is titled *Fatata te Moua* (At the Foot of a Mountain). It is by Paul Gauguin (1848–1903) and is housed in the Hermitage Museum, Saint Petersburg, Russia. There is no relationship outside of coincidence between the title of the painting and that of the book. The collection takes the name of its opening poem; the image was found during cover design.

At the Foot of the Mountain

The first two cantos, as a poem titled *The Metamorphosis*, made the shortlist of the 2014 Blake Poetry Prize. The judges' comments revealed that they had read this as a Buddhist, or Buddhist-influenced poem, written in *terza rima*. This reading is incorrect on both counts.

St. Augustine and St. Epiphanius also referred to Christ as a *scarabæus*.

Canto 1

line 6 — *nell'ombra di una selva oscura*   (in the shadow of a dark forest.)

Canto 2

line 18 — *il miglior fabbro*   (the better craftsman)
See *Purgatorio*, Canto 26, in which Dante is referring to the troubadour Arnault Daniel. T.S. Eliot passed the compliment on to Ezra Pound in a dedication opening *The Wasteland*.

lines 25, 26 — All your feet are fixed feet now: you have been / rebalanced...
See *Inferno*, Canto 1, line 30.

Did I Mention the Dog? (section title page)

The Umberto Saba quote is from poem 1 of 'Autobiography', from *Songbook, the Selected Poems of Umberto Saba*, translated by George Hochfield and Leonard Nathan.

Thirteen Ways of Not Looking at a Blackbird as a Blackbird

For 'way' number 12, see Dante's *Inferno*, Canto 34, eg:

I fear to set it down: I found I was
somewhere where all the sinners were iced over,
Yet seen distinctly, like straws under glass.

> trans, J.G. Nichols.

I, Incitatus

The Rudolf Marku quote is from the poem, Caligula's Horse, translated by Robert Elsie.

Homunculi (Title page illustration)

This is a version of a diagram known as *The Penfield Homunculus*. This diagram was developed from data collected by the neurosurgeon Wilder Penfield (1891-1976), mainly in his work with patients with epilepsy. It is a visual representation of the mapping of body space in the somatosensory cortex of the brain, with the size of each body part representing the size of the area of cortex devoted to it.

Acknowledgements

Poems in this collection have appeared in: *Australian Poetry Journal,* vols *2.1, 4.1* and *9.2*; *Best Australian Poems 2013* and *2014*, Black Inc; *Blast No. 10*; *Blue Dog: Australian Poetry,* vols *1.2, 3.5* and *5.9*; *Land Before Lines*, Hunter Publishers (photography Nicholas Walton-Healey); *Meanjin, vol 79.3;* and *Westerly, vol 49* — my thanks to the publishers and editors. Some shorter poems were featured online on *The Merri Creek: Poems & Pieces, #5, Aug/Sept 2008,* thanks to Kris Hemmensley.

An earlier version of 'I, Incitatus' was published in *Poetileptic* (Five Islands Press, 2005). This is also true of the villanelles 'The Sleeping', 'Villanelle to the Muse From a Disgruntled Poet' and 'The Chamber'. 'Why Homeopathy is Not a Science' was published in *The Brokenness Sonnets I-III & Other Poems* (Five Islands Press, 2011) and appears here partly because it has been reformatted on the page, but mainly because it too is a villanelle, though in disguise; and a result of the same experiments with form (as are 'Moon Mantra', 'Sun Song', and 'His Life as a Sonnet').

'Haloperidol', under the title 'Fragments from a Fragmentation', appeared in *Soft Serve*, the 2019 Newcastle Poetry Prize anthology. 'Heraldic', 'Hospital', and 'His & Hers' appeared in *The Brokenness Sonnets I-III & Other Poems*. They are republished here because the Homunculi series is now complete. Touch wood.

My heartfelt thanks to Philip Salom, Toby Davidson, Mark Reid, Jennifer Harrison and Graeme Miles, for indispensable support and feedback. Thanks to my sister, Lisa McKimmie for the same, and for suggesting and sourcing the Paul Gauguin painting for the cover. I am grateful also to Ross Gillett, Morgan Arnett and, of course, the indefatigable David Musgrave at Puncher & Wattmann.

Five Islands Press, which published my first two books, closed in June 2020 after 34 years of service to Australian poetry, and cannot be thanked enough. My gratitude and respect to Ron Pretty, Kevin Brophy, the late Lyn Hatherly, and all the staff over the years. To document the history of the press and continue to provide readers with ways of accessing the poetry of its authors, the Five Islands website (apothecaryarchive.com/the-5-islands-press-archive) is being re-developed into an archive within the Apothecary Archive. Thanks to Gareth Jenkins for this.

These poems were written on Wurrung, Taungurung, Wurundjeri Woi Wurrung, Wurundjeri and Whadjuk Noongar Country, Australia.

About the Author

Mal McKimmie's first volume of poetry, *Poetileptic*, was published in 2005 by Five Islands Press, Melbourne, and poems from it were broadcast as a program on Poetica, ABC Radio National, in September 2006. The sequence 'The Brokenness Sonnets II' was published in *Take Five 08* (Shoestring Press, Nottingham, UK, 2009), which featured the work of five Australian poets. His second volume, *The Brokenness Sonnets I-III & Other Poems*, was published by Five Islands Press in 2011, and won the 2012 Age Poetry Book of the Year Award.

His poems have been published in numerous literary journals and anthologies since 1990, and he has been active as a poetry tutor, mentor, editor, event coordinator, and lobbyist.

Mal is originally from Perth, Western Australia, and lives in Melbourne. In nomadic pre-poetry years he was employed variously as a deckhand, survey hand, kitchenhand, housepainter, fruit picker, laundry folder and vineyard labourer. He has also worked in welfare, with people labelled as having a 'disability' and people diagnosed as having a 'mental illness'; and has been a part-time ranger working with wild dolphins and visitors at an eco-tourist resort.